c.

www.united-pc.eu

KALEIDOSCOPE TWO

"TALES FROM "THE HOME FRONT"

POLLY ADDROW

FOR PAT AND POLLY

WHO MADE EVERYTHING POSSIBLE

and for my dear friend Lorna

IN LOVING MEMORY

ACKNOWLEDGEMENTS

With grateful thanks to the following who allowed requested images-access free of any charge and free release of copyright for this book

Michele McGeachy from 'Library @vmcc.net
The Vintage Motor Bike Club
Re Image AJS BIKE AND SIDE CAR

Nichola Pass @silvercrossbaby.com
Re Image SILVER CROSS PRAM

also to
J Perrett at SP Computers South West TR112SG
without whose digital expertise the images would not have appeared in this book.

All other memorabilia and ephemera shown are from the personal collection of the author.

ABOUT THE AUTHOR

Polly was born in Bath Somerset and lived there throughout WW2.

With a B.A. (Hons) and TESOL Certificate, Polly has worked for forty years as a Librarian either in the UK or with French and Italian Embassies abroad.

She has traveled worldwide and lived for many years in countries such as France, Italy, Singapore, Malta and Cyprus .

There are currently three books in print under the Kaleidoscope Poetry series with two more books in preparation.

As a proud Celt ,of French ,Irish and Breton descent, Polly feels that the rhyming verse in this series offers a vivid Celtic mnemonic for memory recall, an ideal mode of expression for such poetry.

KALEIDOSCOPE TWO

Tales from The Home Front

CONTENTS

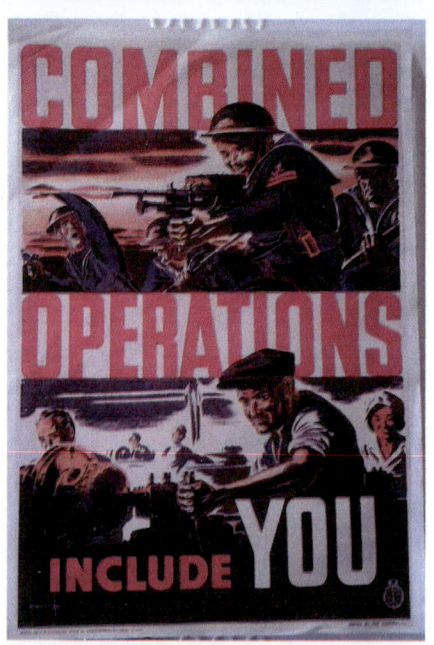

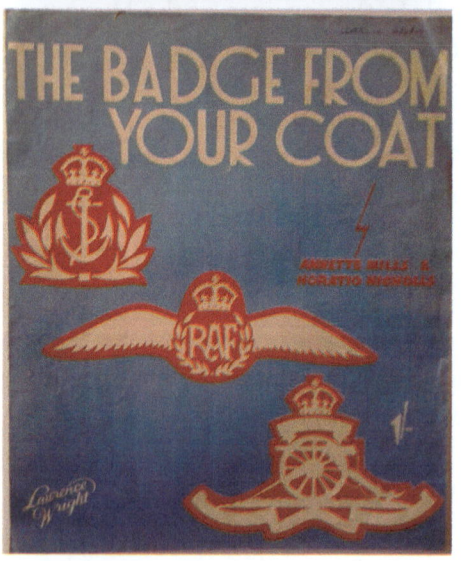

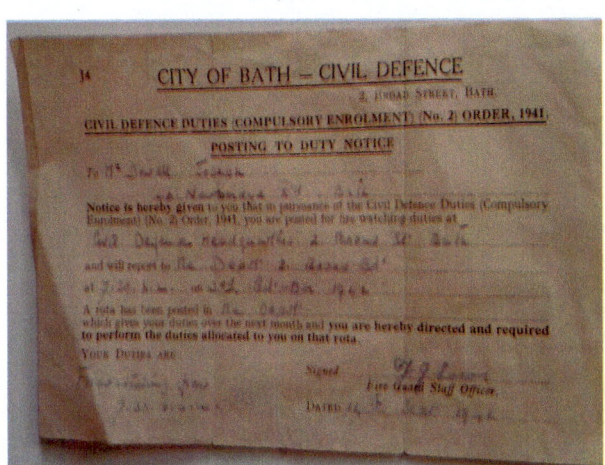

17

UNCLE CECIL

My Uncle came to say goodbye,
he was going off to War.

I was small at the the time,
just three,
but I clearly recall he said
"Remember me" ,
as he rolled me in fun
around the kitchen lino floor.

Then he pushed me in my pedal car
up the path where the orchard lay.

"And anyway," he said, to my dad Pat
"whatever you might say to that,
'tis only right I go you know,
you have a wife and baby here".

Then, pinching me playfully on the ear.
 he turned away with puckered lip
his shoulders held up high

and waived his hand in a last farewell
as he sauntered off- too soon to die.

A lad -just twenty-four, oh how I wish
I'd known him more!

A memory always sore.

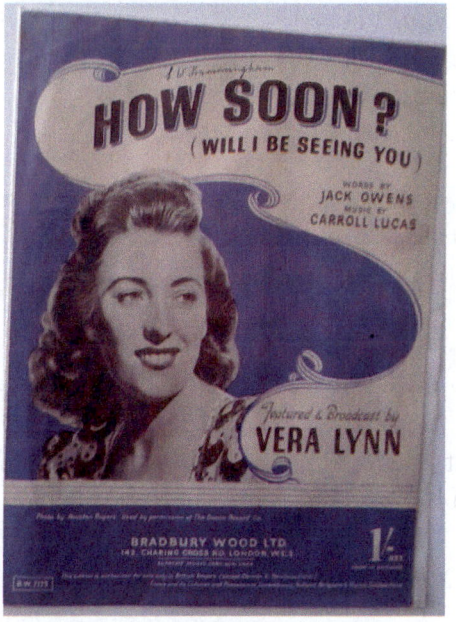

Girls at munitions work

Sobranie Cigarettecase

THE REGLARS

During the War, Aunt Dot
from the "Munitions"
had lots of gentlemen friends

who came to visit "reglar" like"
each and every Saturday night,
 one at a time.

"Say hello to your Uncle Walt" she'd say
or "Jim", or "Jo, or "Pat"-
it never seemed to faze her
to have as many friends as that!

Aunt Dot was always
in tip-top shape
her hair all marcel-waved,
not curly,

her nylons NEW,
no pencilled marks
ran up HER legs,
her calves were held in firmly.

She wore a lot of parachute silk
I saw it as "cammies" on the line
and sported bright red nails
when going out down
the "Hen and Sparrer"

with her half-moons shining
proudly white
as she bent forward to light
her perfumed Sobranies
each and every Saturday night.

Now everyone said
"Best not speak to Aunt Dot
as she has rather fallen from grace".

Which remark I never understood
and took to be very unkind
for as far as I knew,
no-one had EVER said such
to Aunt Dot's face!

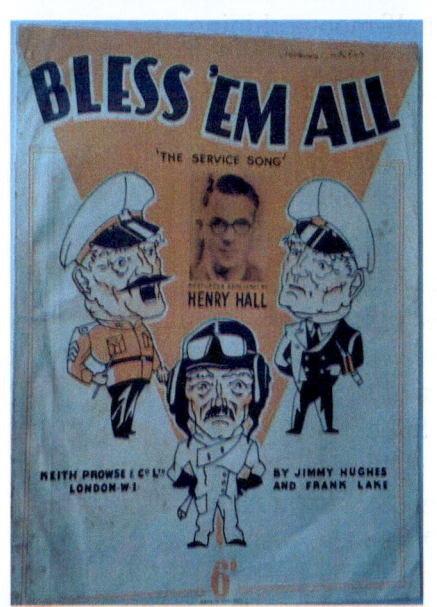

23

KNITTING TO SAVE

For the "War Effort"
Mum ordered "KNIT!"- so we did!

Stitches both plain and purl
passed in a whirl
with 3 needles flashing
for "heel and toe"
-how we longed to see
our brave soldiers' socks
just grow and grow...

But that was sadly not to be
for dropped stitches
were our particular woe
and then we never knew
quite where to go
(needle-wise I mean).

So Mum's carefully unravelled
pullover wool
just kept on unravelling
on our needles still,
cork-screwing and twisting
till it tied itself in knots-
this despite the urgent need for socks!

Soon our over-hasty efforts
were all   undone,

both pearl and plain
twisted like barley-cane sticks,

and grubby too, since our fingers
were often not "up to date" clean
(where Mum had not always seen)!

So our War Effort fell gradually
into total disarray
and we were then thrown out
of the Knitting Circle"'s Knitting Day

and sent off to play elsewhere,
though quite exactly where
no-one seemed too keen to declare.

Three Plain, Three Purl Too Often

"The wife knitted it on the big side, Sergeant, so we're sharing it."

THE ROMAN UNDER THE HOUSE

We found a Roman
buried under our house
on the old Fosse Way
when Dad dug for a shelter,
expecting the War.

"'Tis that gert giant Oolite"
Dad loudly declared
"him that hurled rocks long ago
at his rival over Wiltshire way".

 We nodded in silence,
struck dumb in wonder
our eyes popping out on stilts.

Well, chaps from the Museum
finally came and uplifted
the sarcophagus,
leaving us with a pile of dust
just before the War.

And three years later
they dug nearby,
though in vain,
seeking to lift my pal Daisy
from the rubble
of blitz and scree,

27

a bomb had landed
on her house next door you see.
.Now, the War long gone
we once again dig
the same old spot
though this time simply
for pleasure, in leisure,

for while Daisy and
the Roman are sadly long gone
it seems to me
their essence remains, forever,

mingled   in the soil
we shift and plant
in peacetime spring weather.

AS WELL AS MINE"

LINO
WOOD
RENEW
OLD LINO WITH
LIQUID LINO
FLOOR PAINT
DRIES QUICKLY
CHESTNUT
STONE
SET OF
10
LINO CUTTERS
WILLIAM MITCHELL

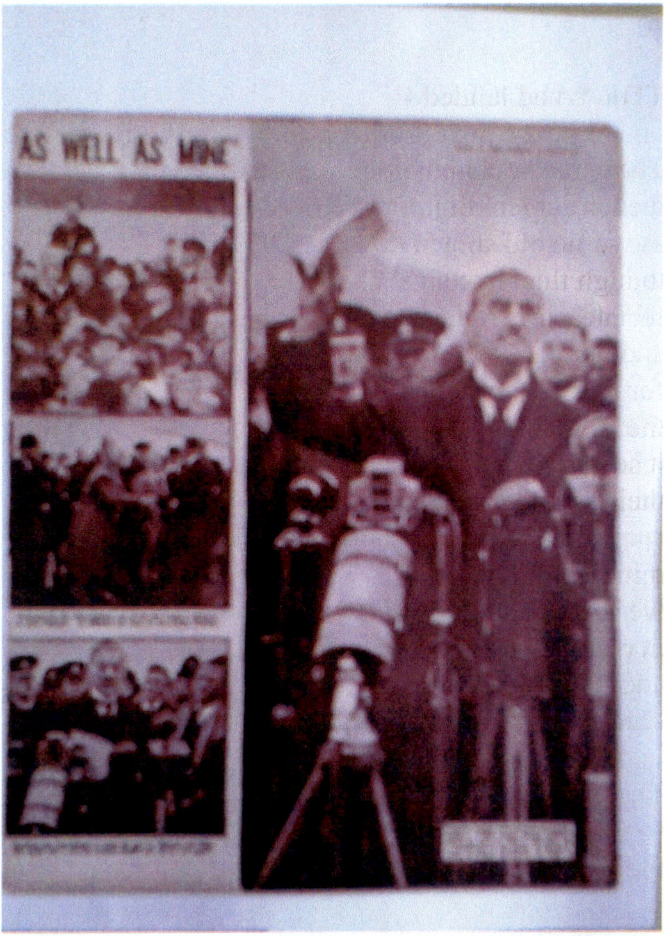

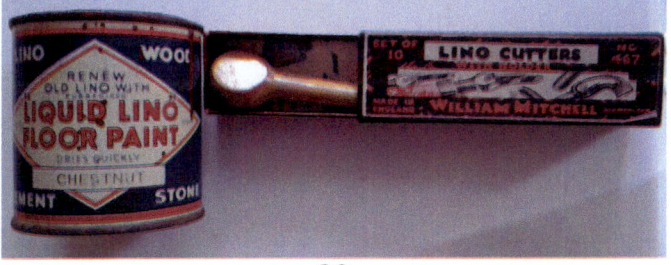

THE "ALL CLEAR"

The Siren sounded as we went to bed,
then bombers droning overhead
as we rushed down, down
to our underground shelter,
all in a push and a shove
and a helter-skelter of fear.

There we were, beneath the parlour
where Dad had dug,
with a nod of disgust,
cursing Chamberlain and his letter".

"Did you hear that?" Dad said,
at every whistle and whine,
and we huddled tight
scared in the gloom of candlelight.

The "All-Clear!" sounded
so we moved back upstairs-
to find we were locked in the house

since the Lino had blast-rolled
up against the walls
stopping us even
from opening the doors!

So we had to climb out
past windows that hung,
still safety-taped in strips
or staggered down the sills.

"That bleeder Hitler's got
a lot to answer for"
moaned Dad chewing
on his black market baccy"

"If I 'ad me way,
I'd charge 'im the cost
of me windol bills,
that would make the mad old sod
REEL unhappy!

31

THE MINISTRY MAN

Aunt Dill was in a fair panic,
"My God" she cried,"we've 'ad it-
the hen-house floor
is sprouting fresh corn,
and that's not the norm,
the neighbours will notice,
just you wait and see"

"It's sprung into life
from the grain left behind-
we'll get the Ministry Man next
at the door,that's for sure"

"And I only fed those chicks
that extra red grain
Jack brought back, under his hat,
from the Docks,
now the damn stuff's taken root
for all to see,

when everyone KNOWS
I only feed my fowls on odds and sods,,
never grain.
Strict about it I am,
so whatever shall I say
to the Ministry man
when he next passes this way!

"Say nowt" shouted Grandad
from the depths of his chair,
"not a clue as to how
that corn got there-

must have blown in from a field,
part of nature;s bounty yield",

and he went back to sucking
on his empty pipe.

Aunt Dill was struck dumb
by Grandad's words,
she shrugged her shoulders high
then paused to look at her pullets
as if bighting on a bullet.

 But when she finally rushed away
I distinctly heard her say

"Grandad's a cunning old codger ,
that's for sure,
I pity the Hun
should he land at our door".

RATIONING

of Clothing, Cloth, Footwear

from June 1, 1941

Rationing has been introduced, not to deprive you of your real needs, but to make more certain that you get your share of the country's goods—to get fair shares with everybody else.

When the shops reopen you will be able to buy cloth, clothes, footwear and knitting wool, *only if you bring your Food Ration Book with you.* The shopkeeper will detach the required number of coupons from the unused margarine page. Each margarine coupon counts as one coupon towards the purchase of clothing or footwear. You will have a total of 66 coupons to last you for a year; so go sparingly. You can buy where you like and when you like without registering.

NUMBER OF COUPONS NEEDED

Men and Boys	Adult	Child	Women and Girls	Adult	Child
Unlined mackintosh or cape	9	7	Lined mackintoshes, or coats (over ⅜ in. in length)	14	11
Other mackintoshes, or raincoat, or overcoat	16	11	Jacket, or short coat (under ⅜ in. in length)	11	8
Coat, or jacket, or blazer or like garment	13	8	Dress, or gown, or frock—woollen	11	8
Waistcoat, or pull-over, or cardigan, or jersey	5	3	Dress, or gown, or frock—other material	7	5
Trousers (other than fustian or corduroy)	8	6	Gym tunic, or girl's skirt with bodice	8	6
Shorts	5	3	Blouse, or sports shirt, or cardigan, or jumper	5	3
Fustian or corduroy trousers	5	3	Skirt, or divided skirt	7	5
Overalls, or dungarees or like garment	6	4	Overalls, or dungarees or like garment	6	4
Dressing-gown or bathing-gown	8	6	Apron, or pinafore	3	2
Night-shirt or pair of pyjamas	8	6	Pyjamas	8	6
Shirt, or combinations—woollen	8	6	Nightdress	6	4
Shirt, or combinations—other material	5	4	Petticoat, or slip, or combinations, or cami-knickers	4	3
Pants, or vest, or bathing costume, or child's blouse	4	2	Other undergarments, including corsets	3	2
Pair of socks or stockings	3	1	Pair of stockings	2	1
Collar, or tie, or pair of cuffs	1	1	Pair of socks (ankle length)	1	1
Two handkerchiefs	1	1	Collar, or tie, or pair of cuffs	1	1
Scarf, or pair of gloves or mittens	2	2	Two handkerchiefs	1	1
Pair of slippers or goloshes	4	2	Scarf, or pair of gloves or mittens	2	2
Pair of boots or shoes	7	3	Pair of slippers, boots or shoes	5	3
Pair of leggings, gaiters or spats	3	2			

CLOTH. Coupon needed per yard depends on the width. For example, a yard of woollen cloth, 36 inches wide requires 3 coupons. The same amount of cotton or other cloth, needs 2 coupons.

KNITTING WOOL. 1 coupon for two ounces.

THESE GOODS MAY BE BOUGHT *WITHOUT* COUPONS

¶ Children's clothing of sizes generally suitable for infants less than 4 years old. ¶ Boiler suits and workmen's bib and brace overalls. ¶ Hats and caps. ¶ Sewing thread. ¶ Mending wool and mending silk. ¶ Boot and shoe laces. ¶ Tapes, braids, ribbons and other fabrics of ¾ inch or less in width. ¶ Elastic. ¶ Lace and lace net. ¶ Sanitary towels. ¶ Braces, suspenders and garters. ¶ Hard haberdashery. ¶ Clogs. ¶ Black-out cloth dyed black. ¶ All second-hand articles.

Special Notice to Retailers

Retailers will be allowed to get fresh stocks of cloth up to and including June 28th WITHOUT SURRENDERING COUPONS. After those dates, they will be able to obtain fresh stocks only by handing to their suppliers coupons. Sizes have been taken, so the incentive of the retailer to buy will be kept during these periods. On quantity of goods which can be received by a wholesaler, intermediate or any one mutually however large his output. Detailed information on be obtained from your Trade Organisation.

ISSUED BY THE BOARD OF TRADE

THE FATTED PIG

During the War
Uncle Ern kept a pig
which he fed on swill-
or anything else that came to hand.

"A ggggirt gggreat thing,'e be,"
he stuttered fondly

"ttttwere a runt you know,
'til Oi took 'e kindly
out out of pity
from the farmer bloke in
fair exchange for a pint of beer.

"Not that Oi be intending
to sell 'e off you know
for that would be the blackmarket.
It's just that Oi've grown to like
the smelly old thing
and do keep 'e purely out of habit!

But when Christmas Eve came,
why- the pig disappeared,
no-one quite knew what was happening.
So as Christmas Day dawned
we gave up the search for Uncle Ern's pig
and settled down instead
to a choice bit of Yule-tide "cracklin"

THE GOOD-TIME GIRL

There was quite a mystery
about our Aunt Dot,
though I never worked out exactly what

She looked rather plain,
but dressed real flash
and seemed to go out a lot-
which was strange when you think
how money was tight
and clothes coupons rarer
than a pig in flight.

But Aunt Dot managed,
no doubt about that,
always sporting the latest fashion hat
with a wisp of a feather here and there

and a hint of a veil across one eye-
as if to keep us in surprise, I suppose,
though heavens really know WHY

And another thing,
for reasons I can but surmise,
(unless she was called upon direct)
her name was only mentioned

in whispers and furtive asides,
with cupped hand in front of lip
and a quick glance around,

as if she might suddenly
pop out of the ground
before our very eyes.

But our Aunt Dot was generous
to a fault,
she loved everyone she knew,
called all the men "Duckie",
"Dearie, "Love"
and was kind to the womenfolk too.

Though another mystery there,
the women did not respond
to her "outgoing ways",
instead they just glowered darkly
and liked her no more
,
which bothered Aunt Dot not a whit,
for she was, after all,
as everyone knew,"rather a flighty bit!

40

THE G.I .BRIDE

"Can't unnerstand that gel,
that I can't"
said Dad pullimg at his "bracers"
and looking for his tie.

"Tweren't as if she needed to,
or there's been some hanky-panky
(leastwise as far as I can tell),
so why she needs
must wed the feller today
is reely as queer as hell"

"Plenty of
sweetheart Tommies
she could 'ave 'ad,
if she waited
till the lads came home
from The Front,

but there you go-
a damned impatient
fllibberty-gibbet,
that's her trouble."

"She'll end up in a fearful muddle
just you mark my words"
and out he went to look for his comb
leaving Mum and me alone.

So Aunt Dot married and sailed off,
with her "you-all Lex"
to become a G.I.Bride
in Salt-Lake City,
humming a ditty and looking rather pretty.

But Dad was right,
she returned alone a few years after
biting her finger-nails
and chewing on her gum,
while her fox cape sadly hung.

"I expected to be his very own Number One "
 she cried,
"not find myself one of THREE,
squabbling all day over the movie show
or what game we might take Lex to see,

oh no- it certainly did NOT suit me!"

And Dad nodded wisely across at Mum
who, forbearing, held her tongue
for what WAS, after all,the point,
when the damage was already done!

THE RED CROSS HUT

Three doors along, next to the Red Cross Hut,
and opposite the Butchers,
there lived a family called TRIM.
There were a Mam and a Dad
(Meg and Peter to us)
and young Mabel,Jack and Jim.

But when the War began to unfold
Pete was called up be a soldier bold,
which turned Meg into a loner,
so as the kids got older
they unfortunately got much bolder
without their Dad.

So Meg took in a "lodger" like
(a smarmy real draft-dodger type
if you ask me)
who paid her one-and-six a week
bed and food thrown in.

Not a very nice chap, come to that,
with one ear up too high
and an ugly lop-sided grin.

The lodger stayed till the end of the war
when Pete came back, unexpected like
one fine and sunny day,

no doubt to joyful greeting
for there were ructions all right,
well into the night, and "goings-on,"
Dad said, "enough to wake the very dead".

And I remember well
Mum telling Aunt Dill
that ""down at Meg and Pete's,
there'd been one hell of a do,
all night through

and no-one seemed
to have gone to bed,
but there were ructions galore
and plenty
of "how's your father" instead".

Then a few months later,
after the lodger had left
another TRIM was born
and people just loved to go and greet him,
for with one ear up too high
and an ugly lop-sided grin
that baby certainly took some beating!

45

THE "SALLY-ANN" AT WAR.

THE "Sally-Anne" had come
to sing hymns and pray
beneath my window one birthday gay
when the Siren sounded high overhead
deafening the Christian cry

and causing all to run awry
towards the Air Raid Shelter
piled up high with sods of grass
to ensure safe delivery
from bombs and blast .

Then the bombs came down
and hit the ground, a deafening
and terrifying sound too fearful for words,
too hateful to bear,
impinging on air in an obscene swear
that echoed round and round
like peas rattling in a can.

All of this rendering
the by now dispersed and shaken
followers of the Sally-Anne
momentarily prayer-less
and quite simply
voiceless to a man!

THE GIRL WITH THE TRACTOR

PICTURE POST

HULTON'S
NATIONAL
WEEKLY

In this issue:

I APPEAL TO THE GOVERNMENT

By EDWARD HULTON

JUNE 21, 1941

Vol. 11 No. 12

3D

THE LAND ARMY GIRLS

My Aunt Sue was a Land Army girl
"not averse to a whirl
in the woods with a "milit'ry" man"
on a bright summer's day
when the hum of bees held sway,

where his hands might safely span
her buckled waist
and his mustachios bristle
all over her face

as he sought to prise apart her lips
with deft little nips,
just as if opening a tin of Spam-
he were a "real tryer"
that milit'ry man!

But Land Army girls are adept
in their ways
and nothing he might try,
(or wish to do)
ever caused my cheeky Aunt Sue
to change
her intended plan:-

A quick kiss for a promise
of "nylons tonight",
a brief fumble permitted

in lieu of lipstick,
packaged war-bright,

a half-hint, a half-promise
of things he MIGHT possibly do
but NOTHING, just NOTHING
a Land Army girl might ever, later rue.

Just a quick escape route
for my Aunt Sue,
"Well, duty calls and all of that,
the land can't wait like you".

So I',m off now Bob, take care,
see you later , toodle-loo!"

THE AIR RAID WARDEN

"Cough Drop" was his name
and "cough-drop" was his nature
for no where would he venture
without his soothing
cherry linctus nectar-
or chewey Gums
or Pastilles thin-
they were all the same
to him.

He went all through
The Home Guard
with his linctus bottle
wedged tight
beneath the webbing of his hat
and whenever things got sticky
well, he just took a swig
from that

before shouting at his neighbours
who had left black-out sheets awry

vigilant in case Jerry might spy out
forbidden lights as he droned nightly by.

"Cough Drop" were rather a puny type
the Medic he had failed to muster,
but at home or on the street
what a terror he was to meet,

with his sickly-fruit linctus breath,
his pop-eyed stare,
his tangled hair
escaping from under his cap
(a horrid sight was that).

And always sucking hard at his
"Victory V and "Victoid Gums"
whilst he idly twiddled his thumbs
or switched to
" Cough Linctus Vector",
to ensure his voice-box was fully primed
the better his neighbours to hector.

DRESSED TO KILL

Uncle Tom was truly a barrel of fun,
for him the battle was never won
without a laugh, a good joke, a pun.

He dressed up too, despite the War
and his antics caused poor Aunt Mae
to pore over the clothing coupons
day and night

"making do"work as best she might
so Tom would always appear
"spick and span",
a true party-going man.

Now Tom were a dab hand at cards,
he loved a gamble or two,
both Newmarket and Loo,
and many a punter had cause to rue
his Dominoes too!.

But his love for sweet Aunt Mae
was his one redeeming trait

and whenever tempted perhaps to stray
by some red toe'd temptress
at the end of his factory day

he would pause briefly to reflect
then with kindness deflect
the offer presented to him.

And the very next night
he would tuck Mae up tight
in the home-made side car of
his beloved AJS Bike,

and despite the fact
that petrol was tight
they would roar off together
into the fading light
for a harmless little spin,

Tom's face all wreathed in a cheeky grin,
for Aunt Mae was truly-"A-OK" for him.

1930

For the man who buys the best.—

A·J·S
Motor Cycles

—The Reason Why—

THE CHAR-A-BANC TRIP

The Char-a-banc trip promised well,
a day at the sea would be swell!.

To Weston we would venture
despite the War, on a "free-for-all"

bolstered with "sannies"
of egg and cress
swigging off ginger-beer-
and all the rest!

But petrol itself proved hard to find,
even the Vicar seemed to mind
when urged
to give up his share,
and offered instead to stay behind
and devote his day to prayer",

Luckily for us,
 "Jim the Tout" was about,
with his kipper tie and Army clout,
so he bartered a seat on the "charrie"
for an old Army pal
who agreed, in return
to part with a jerry-can full of "red".
(which he had stashed ,un-noticed
behind the old School bike shed).

"Strictly in return" he said
 "and as a one-off favour ,
so he might win a wager,

sit on the charrie
next to the prettiest girl,
and then take her for a whirl once
arrived at Weston-Super-Mare"

Which proposition, though dodgy
was quite all-right with us,
none of us saw the need for fuss-

as long as we got there,
well then ,
there was nothing amiss
nor even to declare!

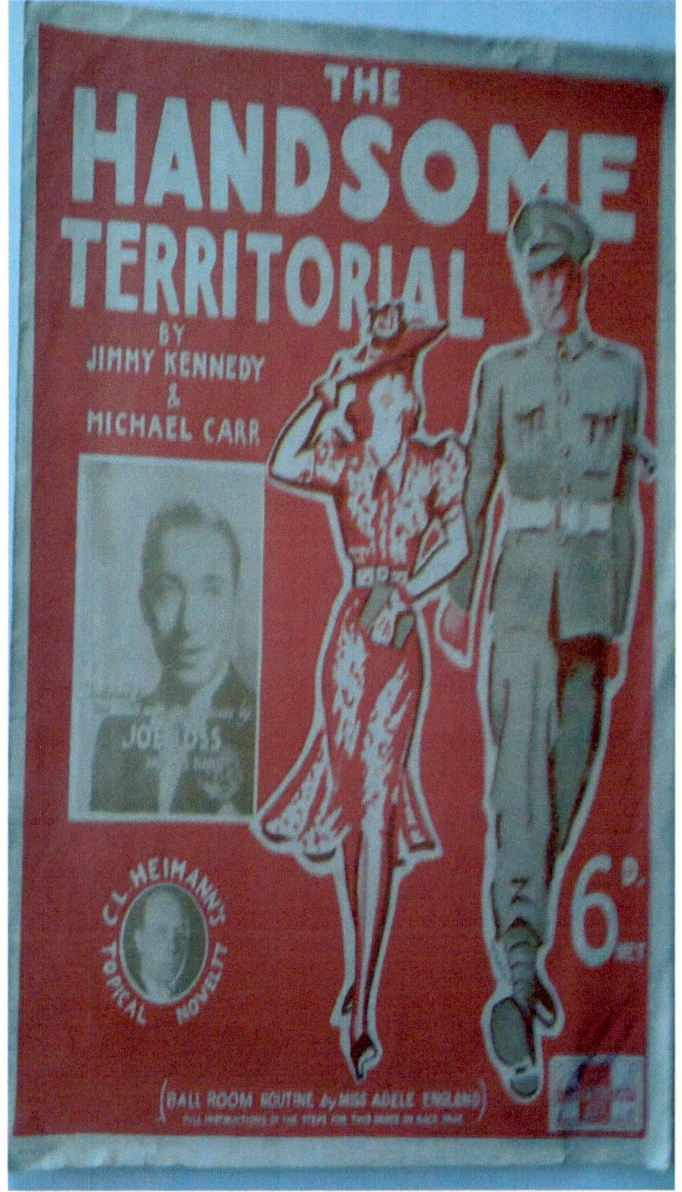

THE UNDERSTAIRS SHELTER

Our cupboard under the stairs
was quite my favourite place,
even where cobwebs and dust
clung tightly, ghost-like
to my face as they brushed by.

One side wall sloped,
stair-shaped, up to a peak,
the other stood square and tall

against which I could lean
with my weight plonked firmly
on the lino-covered floor

stretching my feet out and over
the old trap door that ran
down to the cellar below

and which led down,down,down
twisting like a helter-skelter
to our very own underground shelter.

That had been built in 1938 by Dad
(he being politically sceptic
as well as an honest married lad).

Here, we supposed we were safe
and sound ,free to engage in harmless fun
far removed from our personal
baying Baskerville hound.
the dreaded Hun
and his heavy Gun.

A "G.I." CALLED HANK

Maisie had a friend who was
"on loan" to nearby
Colerne Camp-
a brave G.I. Called Hank ,

who,
although he appeared to have
almost EVERYTHING
(including K Rations
 and candies "on the wing"),
yet never seemed to swank.

So we all took a liking to
Maisie's Yankee "beau"
and invited him to the
local war-time cattle show.

where he thrilled us all,
when, just for a prank
he jumped out before
old Sam Wilson's bull.
tempting danger to the full.

But the bull just lowered his head
and restless,
pawed the ground
instead of churning Hank to dust
as we feared he surely must.

We all held our breath in fear
but Hank -well, he just sort of
lazy- laconic smiled,
(a Texan without any fear),

then stepped neatly to one side
and called for a ginger beer!

And goodness me,
you should have heard the cheer -
it was true indeed,
the Yanks were here!

US sergeants stripes

POLLY'S RED FELT HAT

Her red felt hat was a dream,
not a single seam to show
how war-time funds were low.

A "chic" affair perched saucily
atop neat-rolled netted hair
and beneath it all a face all a-glow
with happiness,since, hatted so,

Polly presented to all in the know
that though times were grim,
with all the men away at the front,
on land or sea or air, and
dispersed heavens know where,

yet nevertheless her hat proclaimed
that she was "keeping up her end"
till the men were brought back
safe home again.

So her red felt hat
was worn day in, day out
throughout the war
for all to see,
Polly's personal badge of bravery.

63

UNDER SIEGE

Great-Aunt Dilys hated the bombs,
she could hear then quite clearly
above the constant fuzz of her
Amplivox Hearing Aid,-

which she deigned to "de-buzz"
in case it was then somehow lost or mislaid,

"Don't worry, my girl!
urged Great Aunt Dilys
to us frightened girls
as things thumped
and crumped outside.

"We know Hitler's
got a lot to answer for,
but should he EVER
land here at my door,

well. I'd give him a blast
from the Rifle my Ted won
at the last village fete-
that'll sort him out,
make no mistake"

"But there,mind, I do wander on so,
but let me say them doodlebugs
will never hold sway

in MY mind,
not with Ted's rifle
hanging on the back
of the scullery door,
oh no. indeed, that's for sure"

And after that declaration
brave Great-Aunt Dilys
went back
to her endless war-time knit
of socks and gloves

leaving her turnip tea
 to get ever-cold
in Tom's old tin mug

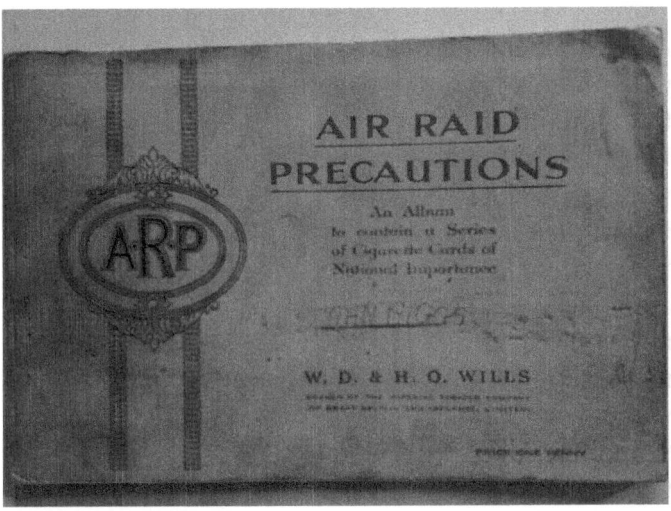

THE DOODLEBUGS

"Them Doodlebugs!"
declared Aunt Millie from Bow
as she searched for a fag
from the depths
of her "crochet"bag.

"Well, they're not the sort of thing
you really want to know'.

Better to be here in BATH
where at least
you are safe from harm
and can have a good laugh
and share as good yarn"

And Millie stopped
to light up,
taking a long drag on that fag.
"Well, them Doodlebugs
were certainly
over-bold back in Bow.

And take my word for it,
not a pretty sight
as they drifted down
with an eery hum
sounding like bread pudding
when it's nearly done.

"Mind you, we certainly did not linger
but dived for cover
in any nook or cranny
that came into view
waiting on each thump
and crump."

"Scared witless we were
most of the time
you can be sure of that.

It turned many a neighbour
as mad as a hatter
trying to avoid
the fearsome splatter
and that's the truth of the matter."

"But there you go,
people are tough in Bow
and not without reason
as well you now know!"

And Aunt Millie returned
to her fag
leaving us all too glad
we were safe in BATH
and not living in Bow.

SHE SOUNDS THE CALL TO SERVICE

SPAM, SPAM AND MORE SPAM

"Spam, Spam, loads of Spam"
piled up high
 in a Silver Cross Pram.
"Just for you, my dear"
said the Spiv
with a leer directed at Mum,

who deigned not to hear his voice,
all deep and over-ripe plummy,
like pouring honey.

So the wide boy persisted
while Mum strongly resisted his spiel,
and she deftly kicked the wheel
of his crummy old van

that would later hide
the then depleted,
yet still prestigious,
second hand
Silver Cross Pram-
when all the Spam
was gone
for a song.

Knowing he would shortly
drive away
at the end of his dodgy day

pockets loaded down
with petty cash.
To load his petrol tank
with Blackmarket fuel

paid for, as a general rule,
from the sale of the illicit Spam
culled from the depths
of his old , much battered
but ever resilient,
Silver Cross Pram.

DIG FOR VICTORY

"DIG FOR VICTORY"
the poster said
hammering its s message
straight into Cousin Den's head.

And, as must be admitted,
his treasured beetroot crop hoard
in size quite simply soared
well above the rest,

was by far the very very best,

nourished on trenches of scrap
carefully purloined
from this and that at Uncle Jim's.

Where a determined Den also
got thin, oh so thin
by hiding away his dinner,

determined to fill his
"nourishing" trench
and turn out a Beetroot winner.

His beet would be
the VERY best,
would simply outgrow all the rest.

His beet would
stave off any ill
far better than
the Army swill
they fed up to each
unsuspecting ARMY LAD.

For as Den already knew
when HIS beetroot finally
started to swell,

well, it was
first class guaranteed
to provide that winning
DIG FOR VICTORY feed.

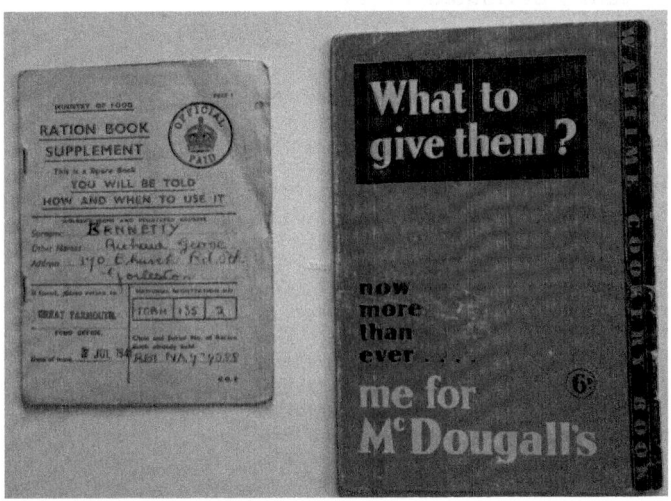

THE SOMERSET AND DORSET LINE

A carriage full of Cockney lads,
our evacuees,
shunted into the arrival bay
of the LNER Station at Bath
one sunny war time day.

They had travelled to Bath,,
packed tight, a fearsome sight,
on the "Slow and Dirty"

as we locals
dared to malign the
"Serene and Delightful"
Somerset and Dorset Line.

They were shouting
and bawling
for all their worth
so we decided to give them

a very wide berth!
.
Each with a string label
firmly tied round the tum ,
an identity kit
from hard-pressed "evacuee" mums.

All ready for a good day out
with no black-out

And they were all
 "full steam ahead"
with their tongues,
make no mistake about that,
with hair all sooted up,
eyes full of coke and grit,
as well as full of
"Vim and it".-

"Cor blimey" I heard one say
as he looked around
at war damaged Bath,
(just a few days after
the Baedecker Raid,)

"They sure 'ave heard from Fritz=
blown half the place to bits".
But his East-end pals
were not impressed
so he was left to trundle
down the platform alone

where he lingered but to hawk
in the LNER Loading Bay,
a Cockney lad forever ,
come what may!

CIVIL DEFENCE

EVACUATION
WHY AND HOW?

PUBLIC INFORMATION
LEAFLET   NO. 3

Read   this   and
keep it carefully.
You may need it.

Issued from the Lord Privy Seal's Office July, 1939

CIVIL DEFENCE

YOUR GAS MASK
How to keep it
and How to Use it

MASKING YOUR
WINDOWS
—

PUBLIC INFORMATION
LEAFLET   NO. 2

Read   this   and
keep it carefully.
You may need it.

Issued from the Lord Privy Seal's Office July, 1939

DOWN BRISTOL DOCKS WAY

Throughout the War,   down Bristol Docks way
(according . that is, to Dad,)
flocks of "vultures" held daily sway
screeching and clucking like hens in a coop.

Sizing up their prospective loot
as dockers disgorged their "prey",
a safe-convoy delivered
at the main unloading bay.

"Get rich quick Johnnies",
Blackmarket Spivs an 'all,
exhorted Dad,rolling his eyes in disgust.

You mark my words, they'll make off
with everything not nailed down
and flog it all for half-a crown!
Never a thought to our brave lads in France!

"I'd 'ave their guts for garters
if I got my way,
but sadly I'm not the Gaffer
just one of the "every day"
so no-one heeds what I have to say"

"It's enough to make a poor man cry".
And Dad paused
to wipe his weepy eye,
then joined his mates for a mug of tea.

WAR TIME DUMPLINGS

Aunt   Rene
from the Red Cross Corps,
despite the scarcities of war
was keen her two nieces
ate well
which often caused us both, to swell!

For she fed us on nothing
but dumplings
whenever she came to stay

and this lead us
to dread her visits
and wish she would keep away,

She fed us on nothing
but suet
till we felt quite ill, fit to burst..

Then when we were feeling
even worse,
sighing at her near-empty purse,
she would send us out
to scrounge for a cup or two
of hoarded " Atora

(as if we had not already
had a plethora).

so she could make another mound
of dumplings firm and over-round.

Meatless dumplings appeared
for dinner,
apple dumplings for tea,
tapioca dumplings for supper-
it was all far too much for sis and me!

"Run Rabbit Run"
Aunt Rene would hum
when her cooking day was done

and although we loved the tune
we never took up the refrain

in case she recalled
what we both deplored
and offered us Dumplings again!

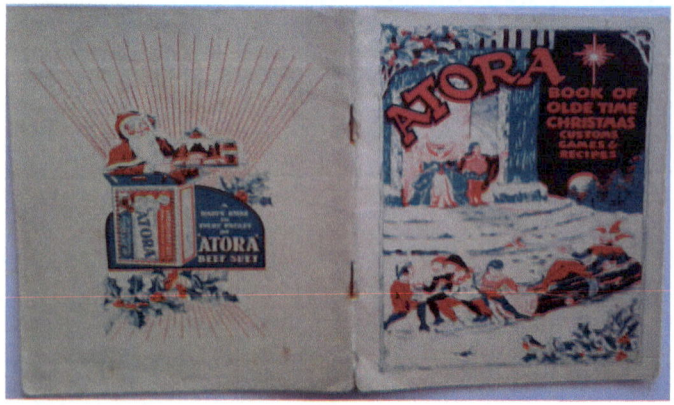

PARODY CHORUSES ON

"RUN, RABBIT, - RUN!"

*

RUN, ADOLF, RUN ADOLF, RUN, RUN, RUN, —
  LOOK WHAT YOU'VE BEEN GONE AND DONE, DONE, DONE, —
WE WILL KNOCK THE STUFFING OUT OF YOU ;
  FIELD MARSHAL GOERING AND GOEBBELS TOO.
YOU'LL LOSE YOUR PLACE IN THE SUN, SUN, SUN ;
  SOON YOU POOR DOG YOU'LL GET NONE, NONE, NONE.
YOU WILL FLOP WITH HERR VON RIBBENTROP, —
  SO, RUN ADOLF, RUN ADOLF, RUN, RUN, RUN.

RUN ADOLF, RUN ADOLF, RUN, RUN, RUN, —
  NOW THAT THE FUN HAS BEGUN, GUN, GUN ;
P'RAPS YOU'LL JUST ALLOW US TO EXPLAIN, —
  WHAT WE DID ONCE, — WE CAN DO AGAIN.
WE'RE MAKING SHELLS BY THE TON, TON, TON.
  WE'VE GOT THE MEN AND THE MON, MON, MON
POOR OLD SOUL, — YOU'LL NEED A RABBIT-HOLE, —
  SO, RUN ADOLF, RUN ADOLF, RUN, RUN, RUN.

*

THE DAILY EXPRESS AND THE A.F.C

On January 1st, 1942,
Dad declared that
"Yes, it were clearly true-
the Daily Express was the very best
newspaper to buy"- and why-

Well, its message
was loud and clear, ,
"To Hitler a Savage New Year"-
to which Dad could only add
a fervent   " Here, here!" "

Then he firmly donned his AFC Hat
(he looked really spooky in that)
and set of to meet up
with his AFC mates

who started their nightly patrol
at the Burnt House Pub gates
where, despite the black-out
and throwing drunks out
at closing time

they had a good laugh,
chuckling over the headlines
in the Daily Express
when their night vigil was done . .

And they all agreed without a single doubt
"What a great headline for that Hitler lout,
what a great Toast"!

For as far as they could see
it would certainly be
NO IDLE BOAST!

PALACE
SUNDAY, NOVEMBER 17th, 1940.

A GRAND

Cine-Variety ENTERTAINMENT

IN AID OF YOUR OWN LOCAL

SPITFIRE FUND

Doors open 5-15. Commence 5-45 p.m.

"The Great Waltz"
MILIZA KORJUS **LOUISE RAINER** FERNAND GRAVET

ALSO THE FOLLOWING ARTISTES

THE PENN GLEE SINGERS
AND PIANIST

| AUDREY CLAPP | DON'T FAIL TO BUY YOUR PROGRAMME IT MAY HAVE A LUCKY NUMBER | DORIS FITZGERALD |

THE LES NORMAN FIVE VICTOR WILLIAMS
GWEN RANDALL

FORD and DOWNS

The New-Avalon Dance Band

84

MYRTLE GROVE

Uncle Ted liked
to offer anyone a fag,
since it allowed him to brag
about his only claim
to war-time fame.

For his "ciggie tin"
bore the legend "Myrtle Grove",
 showing how far he,
as Jolly Jack Tar
had managed to rove
before his "re=pat" to Blighty,

where Ted now chose to act
so high and mighty.

For, as he could, and did boast,
he had bought that tin
way back in '43
when sailing out at sea

aboard the troopship with the
very same name-
his everlasting claim to
naval service fame!

But truth to tell,
no sooner had the Myrtle Grove
sailed into
smelly old Port Teflik

than Uncle Ted had fallen
'orribly, 'orribly sick,
as sick as a parrot in fact.!

So he was soon sent
 "re-pat" to Blighty
in a passing transport plane,
never to go to sea again.

But Uncle Ted would reminisce,
endless,
about his service at sea,

though he fell very quiet
whenever old sea pals turned up,
unexpected like,

to share the latest "sailor" news
and sink a good tin mug of
rum and tea.

87

THE COLOUR RED

Mam just loved the colour
bright and sparky red
and wore it as often
as she could,

despite the frown
handed down
by her elderly Aunts
who would, disparagingly say
in their old fashioned way

"Red Hat, no Drawers"!

But when Mum sported red
she knew her bravest nature
just shone quite through
all the grey and drabness
of her war-time day.

As if she were to say
"Take a look at me,
take a look at me,
see how despite the War
and rationing too
I'm still happy, safe
and ready -for-all.

"So when you see me wearing red
do not on any account fret,
I'm just cocking a snoot at Hitler,
not turned into a trollop-
and doubt I'll do so yet"

SEPT. 1940

STITCHCRAFT

7ᴰ

90

CYRIL, CIVILIAN AIR PLANE SPOTTER

Mam used to frown
when Dad tossed Sis and me
rather recklessly
 up and down
in fun in front
of the Radiogram.

"Just as if, "said Mam,
"baby was no more
than a slice of Spam!"

But this made Uncle Cyril
laugh out loud,
"You're Ok there Pat" he cried.

For Cyril was a careless type,
and a pompous ass.

He just ran on, and on,
"gass, gass, gass"
and never cared
a tinker's cuss
about what
we might all do.

"If Hitler ever landed
in front of Cyril,
well,
he'd be bored to death"
said Dad,

which remark reflected
rather sad I thought
but this remonstrance came to nought.

For Cyril was a Civilian Aircraft Spotter
and regaled us, endless. with his role,

rabbiting on about this and that
lovingly stroking his safety hat.

But with Cyril safely up on the roof
the War seemed more remote
and peace reigned in the house below,
so Mam would wink at Dad and say

"Well, it's all-clear OK tonight
with Cyril away above".

Dad would reply with a grin.
"Quiet it is indeed, my love
since now we can enjoy our day,
with Cyril out of the way

OUR WARTIME MAGICIAN

Uncle Maurice was a Magician ,
he was too flat-footed
to go to War.

He had lost all his teeth at 23,
and in an accident working
at the Jam factory..
had also lost his thumbs.

He took this as best he could
though some jeered out "Lucky Jim"
waggling their   thumbs
right under his nose

or chattering their teeth
till his colour rose.

Anyway he took his magic
all over town
regardless of blackout and blitz

to prove he was not afraid of Fritz,
ignoring the Siren's wail
as buildings around him
were bombed to bits.

People thought Maurice
"funny, peculiar"
him having neither thumbs nor teeth

but he could still roll a Woodbine
between his palms
using a Toy-Town 10- Bob note
taking his affliction as but a joke.

And leaning on any crowded bar
he could conjure up a tin of Spam
as deftly as the Spivvie-man.

So I loved Uncle Maurice
and never missed   his lack of teeth,
nor lack of thumbs, though I must admit
he did not look his best
with his wide and gappy gums.

AT THE FORUM

Cousin Mabel was dotty
about the Stars
she just loved to go to the "flicks"

so much so,
she took a job
as an Usherette
at the Forum in town,
where she could
 indulge her passion
"for free",
every evening after tea.

Which was quite OK
for my sis and me
as we were allowed
to go and sit
without an entry fee.
in the very front row.

Where we gazed in awe at
Deanna Durbin,
hair all swathed
in sequinned turban
as she sang
"The Sheik of Araby",
as clearly as if she were singing
just for my sis and me.

We went to the Cinema
throughout the War,
all through the black-out
we clamoured for more.

We swooned over Bristol lad Cary Grant
we sighed over suave Clark Gable,
and we ALWAYS disregarded
the Siren wail ,
as an unwelcome sound,

till one day we suddenly found
the audience had left the foyer
all in one bound,

and were scrabbling off
to the underground shelter
in a skelter of fear.

My sis and I were carried
along with the crowd,
both of us still singing,
over-loud, the latest song
and dreaming, dreaming on....

thrilled to bits to reach the shelter
safe and sound.
and had not wasted "one-and-six"

My Own Story —

by

DEANNA DURBIN

"Eats!"

I MAY as well confess at once that I am fond of—one thing, and there is such a variety to be had that

NEW LIVES—NEW NEEDS

CINEMA USHER

becomes A.F.S. HERO

LAST YEAR you saw him marshalling the film queues — tall, white-gloved, immaculate. Now the gloves are off all right! He's in the A.F.S., and night after night he answers the call of danger. What an abrupt, dramatic change — and what a tremendous toll it has taken of his nerves and stamina.

IN your strange new Home Front life, remember this, a warming cup of Bourn-vita, out at the old peace-time price, will help you to get the essential body- and mind-restoring qualities from your S L E E P (even though it is interrupted).

Bourn-vita gives, scientifically-sound sleep, and that's the best thing you can take to-day. Bourn-vita is a really food-drink of first class nourishment value, with special nerve-soothing properties that bring deep, very quickly. *No need to analyse if Bourn-vita*

NO SUGAR NEEDED

Get the best out of your sleep with —

CADBURY'S **BOURN-VITA**
Still at Pre-War Price 1'5 PER ½ LB.

WHY BOURN-VITA SLEEP IS HEALTHY SLEEP

THE V-2 ROCKET

Young Sam Sprockett,
the neighbor's son
had been terrified by a V-2 Rocket
while traveling on a train.

And as his mother sadly said,
with a doleful shake of her head,
"He"ll never be the same again!."

"Quite frightened out of his wits, he were
and   he cannot abide any loud bangs
without hiding himself under the stairs!"

"Now he can only moon about, muttering
"Why me?, why me, why me?"
And too scared half of the time
even to finish his cup of tea"

"Don't worry" said Mam in response
to this tale of woe, "we all love Sam so
it don't matter if he acts rather daft."

"Better that, safe at home, than
possibly shipwrecked at sea
left clinging, hopeless to some raft"

His mother thought this through
then brightened up a bit,

"That's very kind of you my dear,
Sam and I really appreciate
your concern especially where
that is often hard to earn!"

So the problem was laid to rest
and thereafter we always took Sam
when going out to play

-but only at simple and quiet games,
V-2 Rocket noises were NEVER
the order of the day.

THE LAUNDRY BOSS

Aunt Lil was a Laundry Boss
and a dab hand
with the Reckitts Blue",

She worked at Bath Steam,
on shift either day or night
and did all right ,

despite blackout and Blitz
when she simply
thumbed her nose at Fritz.

Her girls she organised
like troops into battle
the laundry task was
war-work to tackle.

She always turned up
 "on the dot"
to best supervise
the dispersal of
Soda and Lime,
and to cajole her girls
into what they considered
a thankless task.

So they washed and starched
in time to Vera Lynn's
"Hang out the Washing
on the Siegfried Line"

-which gave them all
a fit of the giggles
and caused perhaps
one or two wriggles
in the ironing fine!

Then, at the end of their day
they settled down
around the mangle
to laugh and chat and wrangle

nibbling on the rare biscuits
their boss had somehow
managed to obtain-
a barter against the cost
of a few freely- washed shirts
I hasten to explain!.

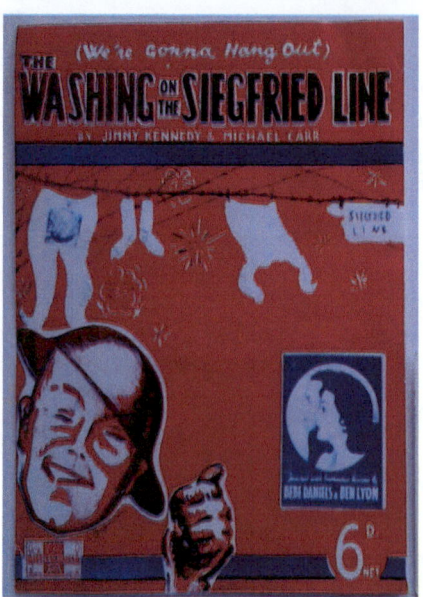

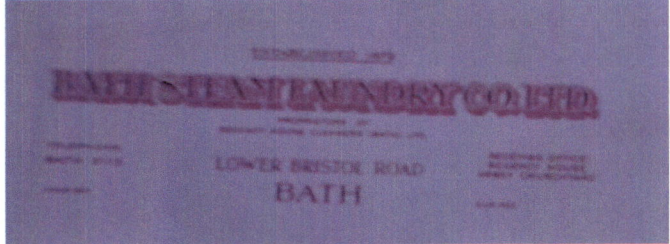

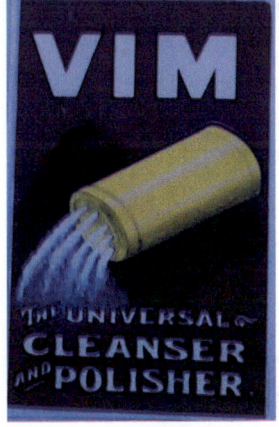

105

THE IDENTICAL TWINS

My Aunties Kate and Bet
were identical twins- as alike
as two peas in a pod.

which was rather odd since
Aunt Kate was timid and quiet
whereas   Aunt Bet was always a riot,
and to put it mildly. Also rather vain.

She would never appear in public
unless she and her twin were dresed
EXACTLY the same.

Until that is, a day when she first
clapped eyes on a WREN,
all dolled up in her No 1 Kit,
and after that, for Bet,
things were never the same again.

For Kate was dragged off to
become a WREN with her sister Bet
and the pair of them disappeared
for weeks at a time,
hardly a moment free
to send us a line or two

"Well, you know dears,
how time simply FLEW"

They came back home
after the Blitz
looking,oh! so spick and span ,

overjoyed to see
we had not been
blown to bits
and were hunky-dory OK,.

With Kate clutching a photo
taken on the Base,
smartly kitted out the pair.
looking more alike than ever,
I do declare.

And identical enough on Parade
to even make their Sergeant swear
"He could not tell one
 from the other"

which fact brought a smile
to the lips of their very proud
mother

WAR TIME SHORTAGES

Mrs Bennetty was her married name
but to us she was just
mean old Aunty Jane

from far-off Gorleston-on-Sea.
she who drank us
completely out of tea!

Jane was never inclined
to help us out
whenever she came to stay
(her Bert being away in France),.

Her ration book
was never offered
to help us out
when food was short.

"I've no intention of
handing it over to you"
she would snort
and Mam would look away
n dismay.

Aunty Jane was never content
just to sit
in the black-out candlelight
preferring to squander our

rationed electric supply
well into the night.

And to use our treddle sewing machine
to run up parachute-silk knickers
to send back home to sell,
or to barter for a supply of ale,

Well, that was our Aunty Jane-
always greedy, always the same.

But when the Baedecker Raid
fell on Bath ,
well that was quite a fright
for our Aunty Jane,

so she upped sticks
back to Gorleston-on-Sea
-very very fast,

which pleased us all at last
and left us free
to share everything again.

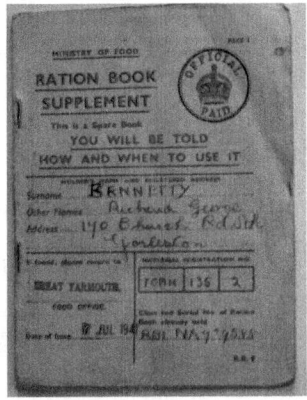

110

A SPIV CALLED BERT

My Cousin Em was rather green
since she was soon taken in
by a spiv called Bert,
who had slicked down
 Brylcreamed hair,

wore a dapper pair of brogues
and had somehow
 avoided the "Call-Up.

He was well in demand
with the girls left at home
(with the lads at the Front)

and in the black-out dark
never looked too flash
or over smart in any
obvious outlandish way.

So a quick kiss and cuddle
from Bert was never more
than a lark to Em.

But things soon went to pot
and Em found out
she was "preggers-like"
which pleased her not a single jot

But when Bert found out,
he was not happy either
buying a ring, he explained
he was prepared to do
despite all the fuss and palaver."

But better to wait a while
till things quietened down
as he was anyway
just called up
to go off to fight,

in fact, he had to leave
that very same night.

"And besides", he said
"it might be better
to leave Em in the tender care
of her fiance Pat,
due home shortly
from the toe of Italy,."

" For as Em must understand,
Pat came first to mind
and anyway,
they both knew in their hearts
that this little fling
had only been a one-off sort of thing."

SCRAP METAL COLLECTING

Our second cousin Sid
was a pig farmer,
which might not sound very grand,
but believe you me
it paid Sid well
to work on the land!

He had started out
as a scrap metal Joe,
not far to go with that
so when the War came around
he soon found himself
in poor demand
since the Government
had requisitioned
all the metal scrap,
so nothing left for Sid in that.

At the Market one day
he spied his chance
and bought up some porkers
on the cheap,
no mean feat to reckon that bacon
would soon be rationed
and hard to find.

So he put his mind
to raising the best porkers
in the local pound
and word of his efforts
soon spread around.

Sid soon made
a packet of dosh.
adeptly wielding
his knife and cosh
so the pigs were unaware of their fate

and he ended up
with an Empire of his own,
sleeping outside the sty
in case any pig might choose to roam.

So, for Sid, the War passed by
in a rather smelly,
but highly profitable way ,
the scrap iron collecting
now quite forgotten
where the nurture of pigs held sway.

WARTIME BIRTHDAYS

Cousin Cedric shared a birthday
with my sister ans me
but there any likeness between us
came to a sudden end,

for he was a first class bore
and greedy too,
always on the scrounge
despite the fact
there was rationing around.

So when birthdav teas loomed
we tried to keep him away,
though somehow
he never missed the day!

He would turn up all kitted out
in his Sunday best,
his eyes all astray
as he tried to grab Mam's party scones
or her spam and cucumber splits

while he bored us quite to bits
on how he would defeat the Hun-
this as her mangled the last Chelsea Bun.

"By golly, what spiffing fun"
he would say,
reaching out
for our greengage jelly
spread wobbly
on home-baked bread.

But Mam would have
none of this lark
and sharply said
"Best go home now Cedric
before the black-out dark"

And he would sadly depart,
leaving my sister and me
to make ourselves scarce
in the cupboard under the stairs

where we would pore over
our birthday cards in glee,

finishing off
Mam's Dundee Cake-
a special treat for us birthday girls
alone you see.

118

THE AIR RAID SIREN

I loved my china Dolly so
her name was Jo,
not Molly , not Milly
nor such like silly, just Jo.

We used to be taken for walks
Jo and me, in the pram together,
by my Aunty Glad,
to her house down the road

for muffin cakes
and milk not too cold-
the latter Jo disdained to sip
being of delicate lip.

Then, one sunny day
the Siren sang
as we were together in the pram
when Aunty Glad was walking us home .

With a sobbed prayer of hope
(for she was "Sally Ann)
Aunty Glad up with her skirt
and ran and ran
winging the pram back home.

.

But the Siren jarred,
we bumped too hard
and Jo flew over the hedge,

and there was nothing left of her
after that but two dear stumpy legs
upside down on a ledge
and her very best visiting hat!

How sad was that.....

THE HOME GUARD

Cousin Jerrold was Chief Clerk
at the Bank
his role in the Home Guard
considered
as nothing better
than a harmless prank,

or rather, as an excuse to swank
when he wore
his Home Guard Hat and kit
to the Forum " flicks" ,

all dressed up to see
"Hellzapoppin" with his girlfriend May.

But on the second day
of the Bath City blitz
his Bank got a personal message
from Fritz-

a series of direct hits
which blew up the building,
threw the Manager and staff,
uninjured ,but very shaken,
clean out of doors

So Jerrold lost his job
and mooched around
in a fit of discontent,
an unlit Craven A
dangling from his lips-

his confidence
greatly shaken all right
try as he might
to appear calm and in control.

But the Home Guard
came to to his rescue
he was made
AN OFFICIAL ADVISOR ,

which meant he could safely brag
about his lucky escape
without having to roam the streets
late,at night,
which scenario suited him OK-all right .

Then Jerrold suddenly changed his tune,
praised The Home Guard to the skies
and,surprise, surprise, his Uniform
was taken down
from its peg in the hall,to be proudly worn
for the rest of the War

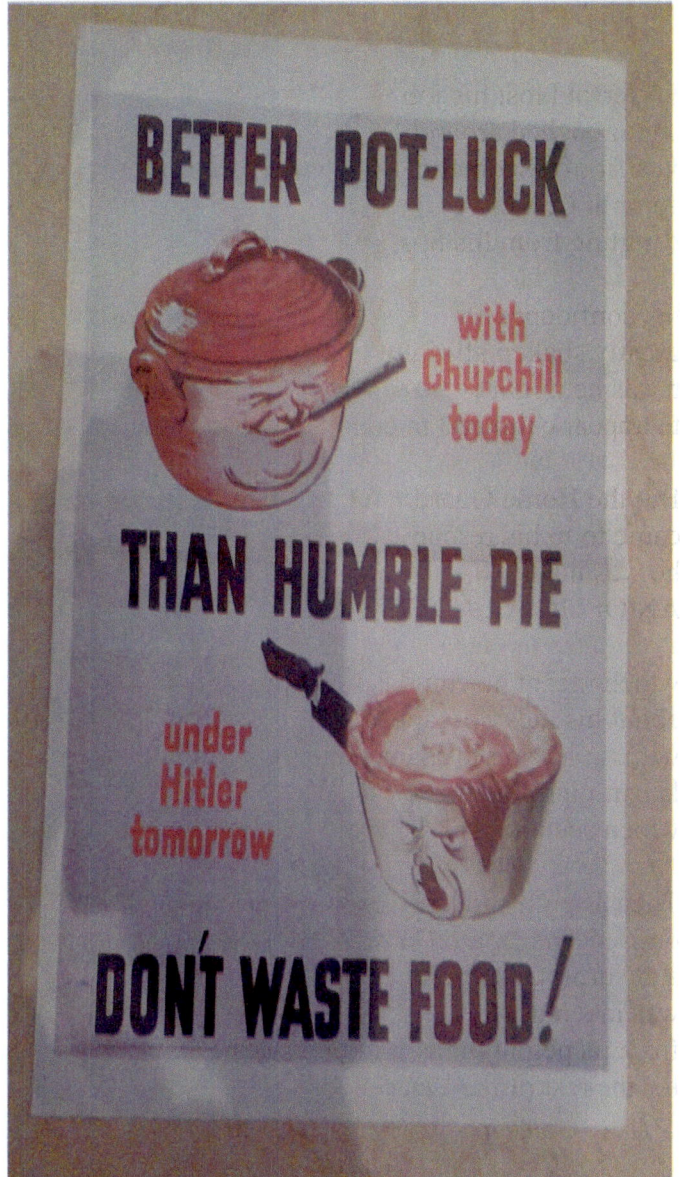

OUR EVACUEES

Our Evacuees were such a tease-
never still for a moment,
drove Mam and Dad
into a regular foment.

Always on the look-out they were,
for some sort of distraction,
for exciting action
here at home,
where we would much rather
have been left,
quiet, and alone to
our own devices
and innocent vices.

But then .
"They were harmless enough,
just hapless victims of the War "-
(or so said Dad)
"and we must 'ave to pity them all".

Even when regular-like
they kicked and teased
our Kimmy-cat
(surely there was no need for that,),
stole Dad's Bristol Docks Pass

or trampled muddy boots
from door to door
all over Mam's pride and joy-
her Mansion-polished lino floor?

They left hob-nail stud marks
throughout the house
though they seemed not to notice
one way or the other,

being too busy fighting
either with me, my sister,
the cat or the dog
or even and quite often,
just each other!

BLACKMARKET JOE

No-one ever admitted to knowing
Blackmarket Joe-
it was "unpatriotic like,"

though all seemed to deal with him
nevertheless
when food and clothes
were scarce on the ground
and there was never enough of either
to go around.

But everyone was always
on the look-out
for a bargain or two, or more.

So Blackmarket Joe grew rich,
as rich as rich could be,
by flogging rationed goods
"Unofficial-like"!,

And never asking more
than he daringly might
for his various
"under the counter deals",

-such as a packet of fags,
a few glad-rags-or even
a spare pair of wheels

It was all the same
to Blackmarket Joe,
so although no-one
supposedly
ever knew him at all,
he was hardly ever
found alone.

Though sometimes
he might be spied
ducking and weaving
as best he might
to refurbish
his deplenished stock,

well away
from the vigilant gaze
of Tom the Bobby in town

anxious, above all
to avoid his
incriminatory frown.

ON REACHING FOUR

"Many Happy Returns of the day"-
how I loved to hear them
say that to me ,
when I had celebrated THREE

For I knew then I would next be FOUR
which I had never been before,
just like THREE.

So my fourth birthday loomed
far far away,
then suddenly quite near
when Uncle Dave
chucked me on the chin
and said with a friendly grin

"You'll be four then next week,
I suppose.
I only hope
the family knows

and you get plenty
of prezzies- like
despite the scarcities of war .

Enough at least
to turn a profit
for Blackmarket Joe.

Lord knows,
he needs the lolly bad enough
to boost the cost
of his wartime escapades,

apart from buying Dolly's
many gin- and -lemonades.

But I was simply puzzled
by this remark
and saw no need to lark about
with Uncle Dave,

so I stuck out my chin, defiant like
and stared and stared and stared
till he finally shoved off upstairs.

Leaving me to ponder
on soon being four-
a place I had never reached before,

though Mam assured me
"I would get there shortly,
despite the War,"

which remark just puzzled me even more!.

BERYL AND THE A.F.S

Beryl was happy enough
to join the A.F.S.
She"just loved the uniform bit,
with her smart navy and blue kit,"

as she wrote to her boyfriend
away at sea- she knew
"he would surely approve her move
and give her the OK too"

She had signed up
without a single qualm
and spent the War keeping busy
especially during the Blitz
as bombing fires took hold.

And she was called upon
day and night"to do her bit",
dousing incendiary bombs
dodging the shrapnel showers.,

hauling people
from fire-engulfed homes
before they too went up in smoke-
survival was certainly no joke!

It was a dangerous muster call
for any girl ,that was sure,
but it suited Beryl fine.

For she knew that when her Bill
finally came back to Blighty
well, then he would be mighty
proud of her role in the A.F.S,

and she had no doubt
that in her smart Navy and Blue
she would certainly always
look her very very best.

GERT THE FLIRT

Dad's cousin Gert
was a terrible flirt
always fluttering her lashes
throughout
all the Red Cross bashes,

and even when climbing aboard
"The Passion "Wagon
which took local girls
up to the G.I. Base nearby.

There she played
the proper vamp
and "acted" ,as Mam said,
"just like a tramp,
with her hair
newly washed in Silvikrin,
Shampoo of the Stars,

and her dress run up
in something thin
so her legs would shadow through!

"And that caused quite a to-do,
and certainly just won't do"
said her Dad Tim
with a doleful shake of his head,

"She'd better look out for trouble
our Gert, for mark my words,
them G.I.'s will have her guts
for garters,
just you wait and see".

"Mind you, I warned her,
yes I did,
but she don't care
a single jot whatever might
befall her lot.

I hesitate to say,
but she be so flighty
it do fair take my breath away."

So pondered a worried Tim
shaking his head in dismay
as he made his way,
sorrowful, to bed,

absently dropping the front door latch
(as was his usual habit)

which simply meant Gert
was locked out for the night,
and encouraged her
in her bad habits ..

Shirt maker

by Wolsey

WOLSEY LIMITED LEICESTER

SAVE! . SAVE!, SAVE!

"Save, Save, Save!
All the Posters said
their message dancing before our eyes
and hammering into our heads
before we went, sleepy, to bed.

"SAVE FOOD!,, SAVE PETROL!,
SAVE TYRES, SAVE CASH"-
they exhorted-
as if we had enough of any of that
to stash away for any needy day!

Why, the Bombs might fall
at any time
and blow us all to smithereens
fat chance we had to save-
we never had the means!

But somehow, "SAVE" we did,
as best we might,
saving on water, fuel and light
all achieved by acting " careful tight".

Since we all knew that by saving
as hard as hard could be
that we were helping Churchill along,
upholding Churchill's "V-"

the very symbol we hoped
my Sis and me, would herald
our final, well- earned ,
hard-worked- for,
and anxiously awaited,
glorious VICTORY.

MAKING DO

Mam was a dab hand
at "making do"
and come to that, I tried hard too.

We all scrimped on food,
endlessly mended our clothes,
saved whatever we could,
made chairs from old fire-wood.

In our home
we turned sheets to middle,
wove shoe laces from twisted string
and every scrap of dried old bread
was milk-soaked
to stop us becoming too thin,.

And next door to us,
old pots and pans
too useless for scrap

were turned into
seed trays by our Uncle Jack
who was ever proud of his seedlings
nurtured with loving care,
pricked out to grow apace.

All so he could brag
about his endeavours
to GROW FOR VICTORY
and not lose face
in seeing what we had achieved
for the Make- do Campaign .

So neighbourly rivalry thrived
all in aid of winning the WAR
and we renewed our efforts endlessly,

sometimes even forgetting
to stop for a chat and a
much re-stewed cup of tea.

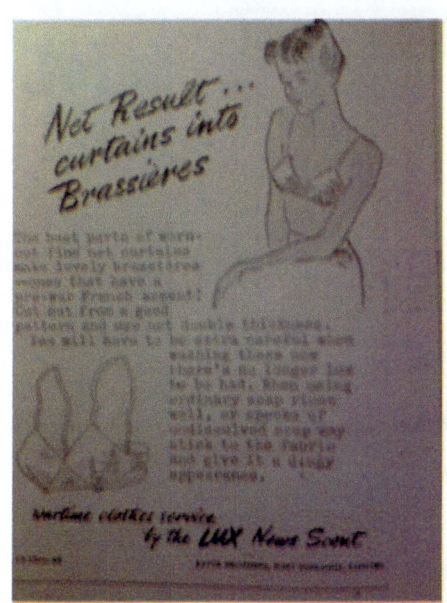

141

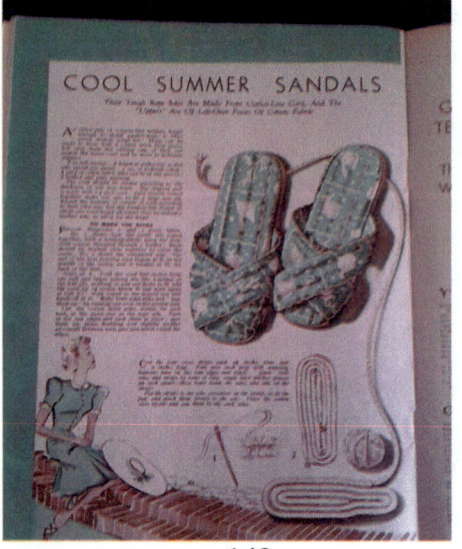

GAS MASKS AT SCHOOL

Our Gas Masks were not much fun
despite the practice run
"On how to wear during an attack"-
it scared us even to think of that.

Mr Wells the Headmaster
summoned us all
to the Hall, where we huddled,
apprehensive, about it all

gazing up in awe at the Cane
which hung in warning
for us all to see, high above
the |Schoolhouse Clock, which
suddenly struck four
time for home and tea.

Now my good pal Jim,
being a bit of a spark
simply blew raspberries
into his mask
which rolled around like one
continuous very rude fart,

causing us all to laugh
and Mr Wells to take Jim
seriously to task.

And the swish of the Cane
frightened the Infant Class
and they all cried for their Mums,
with the smell
of their Mickey Mouse masks
simply upsetting their tums.

But we had to practice
each and every day
"In case Hitler chose
to drop sudden-like by
gassing us all in a twinkle of an eye"

So we persevered
with that sobering thought,
coupled with the image
of the terrifying School Cane

which we did not wish
to see taken down
EVER, EVER AGAIN

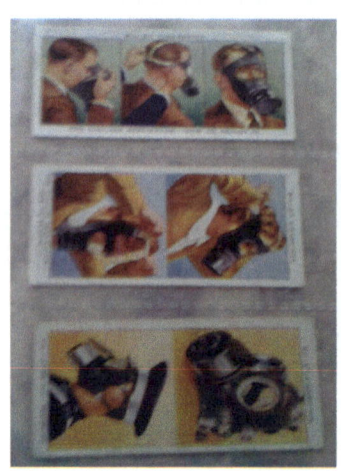

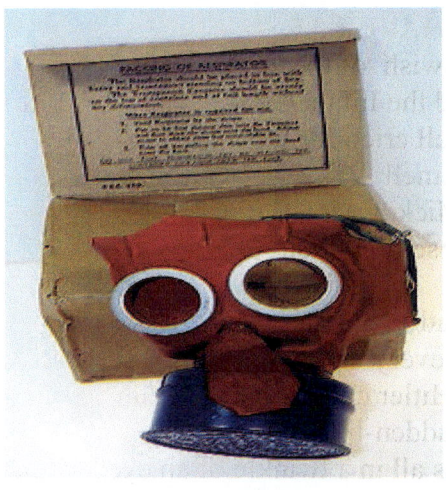

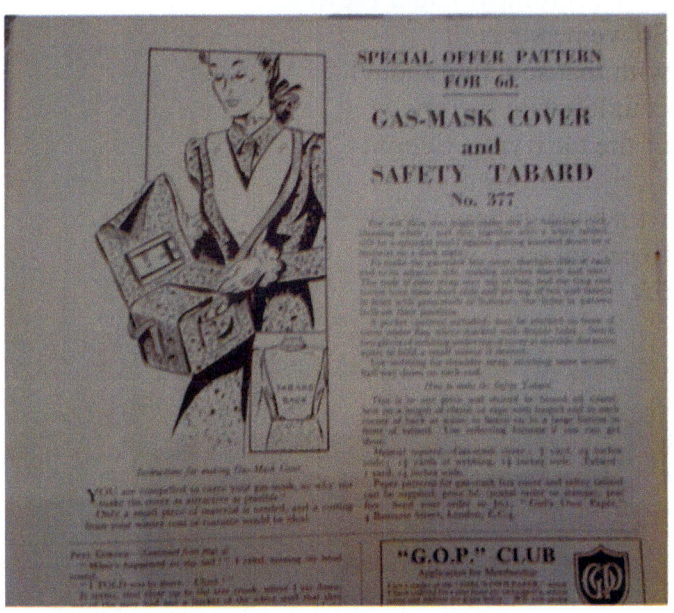

WALLS HAVE EARS!

"BUTTON YOUR LIPS!",
"WALLS HAVE EARS!-
such were the fears
put about during the War
by the Ministry of Defence

and these seedlings of advice,
once implanted, steadily grew,
rooting deep in the soil of the brain

as sure as a draught of
strong scrumpy Cider brew
will repeat there
time and time again.

So we all went about
looking constantly
over the shoulder,
whether young or old,
or even that much older!

Our fingers we stuck tight to lips
in cautionary mode
as we chatted of matters
simple or bold

Determined we were
that Hitler's spies
would never be party
to any surprise we might
propose about the War,

our Victory through silence
thus safe guaranteed,
of that we were
"Certain sure".

151

> ‘ In the long years to come not only will the people of this
> island but of the world, wherever the bird of freedom
> chirps in human hearts, look back to what we've done and
> they will say 'Do not despair, do not yield to tyranny,
> march straight forward and die if need be – unconquered ’
>
> **WINSTON CHURCHILL**

V.E.DAY CELEBRATIONS

We danced all night,
or so it seemed,
hair all crimped in "Toni" wave,

socks dangling down from our knees,
Alice hair-bands flying all away-
it was V.E. DAY

On Dad's shop front
we plugged in a "grammy"
plus a ' tannoy,' all set at the ready.

We kitted out stalls
with hoarded bread,
slithers of cheese,
bowls of home made mushy peas

and even a few isinglass eggs
carefully thrown in.
And oh! What a glorious happy din.

The Vicar's wife
waltzed with Mr Sharp,
a great big Victory rosette
plonked over her heart
so proclaiming loud and clear
"We've won, we've won, we've won!

The Air raid Warden joined it too
no longer obliged to shout
"Oi, put that dratted light out"..

Mrs Postlethwaite, our Ministry Lodger
smiled graciously when asked to dance
by our local butcher, Mike,
though she pursed her lipstwhen
squeezed (as she thought) rather over-tight.

There was ginger-pop fizz for one and all,
Aunt Dill had made it
in the shed behind her store,

and knitted purl and plain streamers
(made by who knows who)
were hung as bunting over the queue
around the outdoor loo.

And I saw Mam take Dad's hand
and squeeze it tight, then tighter,
Hitler was finished, sent to Hell
- good riddance to the wicked blighter

We laughed, we cheered,we clapped
and sang to Anne Shelton and Vera Lynn
our heads now a spin of joy-
we had WON,
NOW we could have FUN!.

So I finally crept away,
fully tired out
to sit in the dark
with our "Eyetie" Prisoner of War

who came every day
of the working week
from the Prison on Entry Street,
ordered to clear up debris and scree.

And I looked up to see him
crying down
on dim curl-edged photos
of his family, way back in Italy.

"Mama mia!, 'is finished now" he said
with a nod of his head
and his hands clasped in prayer.

And I took his hand to share the joy,
for we both knew the War was ended,
we had no more need to fear,
V.E.DAY was here-

PEACE at last!!

Vol. 11. No. 12   PICTURE POST   June 21, 1941

The Man on Whom Everything Depends: Winston Churchill, Britain's Leader in the Most Critical Hour of All.

AN APPEAL TO THE GOVERNMENT

8th June, 1946

To-day, as we celebrate victory, I send this personal message to you and all other boys and girls at school. For you have shared in the hardships and dangers of a total war and you have shared no less in the triumph of the Allied Nations.

I know you will always feel proud to belong to a country which was capable of such supreme effort; proud, too, of parents and elder brothers and sisters who by their courage, endurance and enterprise brought victory. May these qualities be yours as you grow up and join in the common effort to establish among the nations of the world unity and peace.

George R.I.